5 BEST PRACTICES FOR **UNLOCKING** YOUR EMPLOYEES' **HIDDEN POTENTIAL**

WHAT'S IN IT FOR ME?

Njanja Mathu Gakuru

Copyright, Legal Notice and Disclaimer:

This publication is protected under the US Copyright Act of 1976 and all other applicable international, federal, state and local laws, and all rights are reserved, including resale rights: you are not allowed to give or sell this book to anyone else.

Please note that much of this publication is based on personal experience and anecdotal evidence. Although the authors and publisher have made every reasonable attempt to achieve complete accuracy of the content in this guide, they assume no responsibility for errors or omissions. Also, you should use this information as you see fit, and at your own risk. Your particular situation may not be exactly suited to the examples illustrated here; you should adjust your use of the information and recommendations accordingly.

Any trademarks, service marks, product names or named features are assumed to be the property of their respective owners, and are used only for reference. There is no implied endorsement if we use one of these terms. The names and situations used in this book are fictional and not real people. If any name or situation sounds familiar or similar to you, it is purely coincidental.

Finally, nothing in this book is intended to replace common sense, legal, medical or other professional advice, and is meant to inform and entertain the reader.

Copyright © 2011 Njanja Mathu Gakuru. All rights reserved worldwide.

5 BEST PRACTICES FOR **UNLOCKING** YOUR EMPLOYEES' **HIDDEN POTENTIAL**

WHAT'S IN IT FOR ME?

Njanja Mathu Gakuru

DEDICATION

To my amazing husband Peter Gakuru. Thank you for believing in me.

To my mother Lillian W. Mathu and my siblings, Njeri Njenga, Ngugi Mathu and Kariuki Mathu, for the love and support they have given over the years.

And to my late father Eliud W. Mathu for the lessons we learnt from his actions: confidence, diligence, motivation and hard work are the keys to success.

I thank God for making this all possible.

ACKNOWLEDGEMENTS

Thank you for the role you played in making the book a success. I could not have done it without you.

Kristina Killgrove, freelance editor.

Denise Prichett Photography

Duolit Publishing LLC.

TABLE OF CONTENTS

Part One:

GETTING STARTED RIGHT

INTRODUCTION

If you have a task to perform and are vitally interested in it, excited and challenged by it, then you will exert maximum energy. But in the excitement, the pain of fatigue dissipates, and the exuberance of what you hope to achieve overcomes the weariness.

- Jimmy Carter, 39th President of the United States

On Jessica's first day at work, she felt confident and ready to take on the world. You know that feeling? She walked into orientation, pleased to meet other new employees. Jessica had already had been introduced to a few people in her department and had spent time 'shadowing', sitting with different people all day, watching what they did and trying to get the most out of it.

Jessica looked through her manual and Human Resources forms. The HR representative was helpful with the forms and covered them in detail, spending two hours going over the material. As the second hour came to a close and the representative dismissed everyone, Jessica began to wonder: What is this company all about? What is their history? Who are the leaders? Wait a minute, where is the bathroom? One question led to another, and as a new employee she felt she could only ask so many questions. Jessica had done some research on the company before orientation, but she felt it would have made a big difference to hear someone reiterate the important things about the company, its mission, vision, goals, and opportunities.

How many times do employees arrive at their new place of work, excited and ready to begin, only to be frustrated by the lack of communication? How often is their training put on the back burner?

When that energetic employee you interviewed seems like a totally different person two months down the road, do you wonder what happened? Is it possible to keep that excitement and perhaps even increase it so as to turn him or her into a learning and high producing employee? You can play a part by starting them right and taking the time to discover the things that motivate them to reach their potential.

Corporations today can no longer disregard the importance of on-boarding, recognition, and creating opportunities for growth. Employees are truly a company's most valuable asset; investing in them needs to be a priority for a company to stay competitive. Jack Welch understood that and made learning a priority at GE. Employees at GE were encouraged to be creative in solutions and ideas, and they were rewarded when their commitment to learning led to revenue or productivity increases.

Managers today cannot disregard the career goals of their employees. Nurturing the drive of these employees will lead to their working for the company, not against it. That is the ultimate advantage for improving performance, increasing productivity and retaining employees.

What is your current situation? What do you want to accomplish?

Through personal experience and interviews with both employees and employers, I have learned how employers can work to meet the needs of their employees so that both parties benefit. If you are reading this book, you have a desire to make a difference and you can make a difference. In this book, I show you how to help new employees stay motivated not only during their critical first few days of employment but also throughout their career.

First, identify what is lacking in your current situation, and then define what you want to accomplish to ensure that you are moving in the right direction. You may be looking to improve your on-boarding process, training and development, employee feedback and communication processes, or employee participation within the organization as a whole.

No matter your goal, it is imperative to focus on creating and maintaining a positive attitude within your organization by:

1. Making your new employees feel welcome
2. Helping them reach maximum productivity as quickly as possible
3. Reducing stress
4. Increasing job satisfaction

5. Helping them reach their potential

It is your responsibility as their manager to ensure that your employees are successful. You would be surprised at how little it takes to do this. Little things that may not seem important to you can be essential to an employee's job satisfaction.

In the following pages, I discuss five best practices that will help you unlock your employees' hidden potential. It is important to hire talented, motivated employees, to make sure that you get your new hires started right, and to do what it takes to retain your best employees. On-boarding, career development, recognition, and communication are extremely important to your employees. These topics are covered in depth so that you can get more from your employees by giving them more.

Part I of this book talks about motivation and the importance of incorporating an on-boarding program that will help new employees reach productivity or competency quickly. You will learn the importance of preparing for your new hires, as well as some important topics to cover with them early in the game and different methods you can use for on-going learning and development. Part II talks about understanding your employees and their career goals in order to improve productivity, increase teamwork, and encourage employee participation.

PRACTICE I: *MOTIVATION*

"Motivation is described as a need, desire, or a want that serves to activate or energize behavior and give it direction."

- Kleinginna and Kleinginna, 1981

"Motivation is also defined as the psychological feature that arouses an organism to act toward a desired goal."

- TheFreeDictionary.com

In order to successfully motivate employees, you need to create a reason or a situation that will drive them to do what's required of them on a daily basis. At the same time, you want to remove any distractions that could prevent them from meeting their goals, keeping in mind that distractions can also come from negative employees. A motivating environment or lack thereof will impact productivity, absenteeism, employee turnover, and customer satisfaction.

Necessary ingredients for fostering a motivational environment have been put forth by Malone and Lepper (1987), who listed seven factors that can be used to motivate learning. As a manager, understanding these factors will help you create a winning atmosphere. You will see in this guide evidence of how these seven factors apply to the work environment.

Think about your direct reports and try to place them into one of these categories of motivation:

1. Challenge
2. Curiosity
3. Control
4. Fantasy
5. Competition
6. Cooperation
7. Recognition

CHALLENGE

People are motivated when they are working towards meaningful goals that have some level of difficulty. Employees want to work towards a goal, but they also need to know that they can meet those goals. For these employees, you should:

- Establish SMART (Specific, Measurable, Actionable, Realistic, Tangible) goals for them. The goals should be challenging yet attainable.
- Be sure to communicate those goals to them often.
- Provide them with feedback on their performance.

CURIOSITY

Motivating people by stimulating their curiosity is not as simple as it sounds. Most employees have specific tasks to complete, and at some point these tasks become second nature and almost mindless. It's important to find ways to pique curiosity in order to attract the employees' attention and help them remain engaged. Engaged employees tend to be more productive.

CONTROL

Everyone wants to feel that they are in control of their destiny, at least to some extent. Provide an environment that allows your employees to feel in control of the outcome of their daily tasks and the decisions they make. As a manager, you can provide this feeling by:

- Letting them know that what they do makes a difference by indicating how it relates to other departments within the company.
- Allowing your employees to choose their daily start time if flexible schedules are available. Companies that embrace flexible work schedules tend to have an advantage over those that do not.
- Allowing them to choose what they want to learn in addition to their required training.

FANTASY

When you imagine yourself on the beach on a cold snowy day or when you imagine yourself closing a large deal on your way to a sales pitch, you are challenging your mind with an alternate perception of reality. These fantasies can make a difference in the way you perceive yourself and your situation. Encourage your employees to imagine themselves as Team Leads or being promoted to different roles if such career paths are available. While this may not apply to all situations or employees, allowing employees to imagine a different path can be a great way to help them loosen up and get motivated.

COMPETITION

A little healthy competition doesn't do any harm. When using competition, keep it light and fun. Competition helps increase self-esteem because we as humans gain some satisfaction by comparing our performance to others'. You must be careful with this process, though, because:

- Not everyone is motivated by competition.
- Losing can de-motivate people more than winning motivates them.

COOPERATION

Many people are motivated by helping others achieve their goals. One way to encourage cooperation is to create opportunities for senior members of the team to coach newer members on certain tasks. Assigning such a task lets an employee know that you trust them and their work. That alone increases their self-esteem, and they know that their work makes a difference.

RECOGNITION

This is one of the most common ways to motivate employees. Simple gestures such as a pat on the back, plaques, gift certificates, dinner coupons and time off are great motivators. Recognition shows that you care about what your employees do and that you are well informed. When recognizing employees:

- Use verbal recognition as often as possible to appreciate employees' accomplishments.
- If using tangible gifts to recognize accomplishments, ensure that you deliver the gift yourself and let them know specifically what it was for.

Motivation is important for jump-starting your employees into action. Your first step toward fostering a motivating environment is to identify which employees are motivated and which ones are not. It is critical to understand the differences between motivated and unmotivated people so that you can more easily point out the dominant character in each of your employees.

The Motivated Person	The Unmotivated Person
Sets goals both long and short term.	Is directed by what others think.
Has high self-esteem.	Has low self-esteem.
Is positive.	Thinks negatively.
Takes responsibility for his/her own actions.	Blames circumstances.
Focuses on strengths.	Focuses on weaknesses.
Has successful habits.	Has bad habits.
Willing to go the extra mile.	Does just enough to get by.
Welcomes new challenges.	Resistant to change.
Contributing team player.	Does not contribute.
Is pleasant most of the time.	Is usually in a bad mood.

Which of your employees fit into the motivated column and which fit into the unmotivated one? Do you think you can change an unmotivated employee into a motivated one? How are they affecting your team's overall attitude and performance?

Find out what motivates your employees, keeping in mind that everyone is motivated by different factors. In other words, you need to understand how each team member is motivated to be able to create some balance. You cannot please everyone, but you want to understand what the majority of your employees value the most so that you can tap into that energy, that hidden potential. To find out what motivates your employees:

1. Ask them what they value. This will give you insights into which of the seven motivational factors might be high on their list.
2. Test one of Malone and Lepper's factors on an employee. For example, if you think that a challenge might help motivate a specific employee, try using that factor.
3. Get feedback from your employees and check with them about their feelings.
4. Do not introduce something into the work environment that is counter-productive to your goal.

As you create a motivating environment, you will help your employees reach their potential.

PRACTICE 2: ON-BOARDING

"An organization's ability to learn, and translate that learning into action rapidly, is the ultimate competitive advantage."

- Jack Welch, former GE chairman and CEO

On-boarding is the process of hiring smart and helping new employees become acclimated to corporate processes and culture as quickly as possible. It involves taking advantage of the new employees first 90 to 100 days (or more) in order to help them become productive members of the organization. On-boarding is a very important factor to consider because it shapes the future of your employees within the company, the direction of your department, and how well you meet your goals.

Jimmy, a recent hire, had a short and productive first day. He met with his manager in the morning to briefly discuss his tasks. He received an online coursework assignment and was introduced as a new team member. On his second day, Jimmy met a few members from another team that he would be working closely with and then shadowed the rest of the day. This gave him an idea of the culture, pace of the environment he would be working in, and a little about the expectations of his new team. On his third day, Jimmy was hopeful that his computer would finally be ready for him and that the phone would be re-programmed with his name in the voicemail. Two weeks later, though, Jimmy had no computer and was still shadowing. He had a list of online courses to complete and snagged an available computer whenever an employee was out of the office. Jimmy received no indication of an upcoming orientation or formal instructor-led training. Before his third week had come to a close, Jimmy left the company.

Some companies treat their employees like Jimmy, and this inattention to new employees happens in many different industries. Not all employees are as quick to leave as Jimmy was. Patient employees will complain but will not let a situation like Jimmy's change their attitude towards you or the company so early in their career. In order to avoid making the mistakes that Jimmy's manager did, it is imperative to design an efficient and effective on-boarding program. The following steps will take you through creation of a thorough and effective on-boarding program.

1.0
PREPARATION

You spent time finding and hiring a motivated candidate, but you also need to ensure that their introduction to your company or team helps them become an effective and satisfied employee. There are four important steps to getting your employees started right:

1. **Preparation** - aimed at reducing first day jitters and making the employee feel welcome.
2. **Orientation** - aimed at providing basic information that will allow the employee to be productive quickly.
3. **Training** - aimed at increasing job knowledge and therefore job satisfaction.
4. **Evaluation/Follow-up** - for the purpose of receiving crucial feedback about the on-boarding process.

You cannot keep an employee motivated if you did not hire a motivated employee in the first place. It is therefore imperative to have a solid hiring process. Consider these important suggestions for hiring a good candidate.

- **Collaborate with Human Resources** (HR)

Provide HR with the position's job description and have them do the initial screening. Ensure that your job description includes not only the skills required for a specific position but also the attitudes necessary to be successful, such as friendliness, good listening skills, patience, and so on. One mistake that some managers tend to make is hiring solely based on experience and education. It is easier to teach a skill than to change someone's character, so aim to hire a well-rounded employee in terms of the qualities you are looking for. HR can assist you by weeding out the candidates that do not fit the job requirements by reviewing their resumes and conducting a phone interview. This will allow you to be involved with interviewing only those candidates that closely meet the job requirements. Phone interviews conducted by HR to weed out candidates may not apply to all positions, such as programming or engineering, but they may work well for customer service positions. Use your judgment based on past experience - yours or others'.

- **Conduct at least two personal interviews**

Two interviews will allow you to get to know more about the candidate. Try to schedule these on different days of the week and possibly at different times of the day (morning and afternoon). Your goal here is to get to know the candidate's temperament and attitude to ensure that they are the right fit. No one person will behave exactly the same on two totally different occasions or situations. It will also allow the candidate to loosen up.

- **Introduce the candidate to the team**

This allows your team to feel involved in the hiring process, which in turn makes them more inclined to be accepting of the new employee when and if they are hired. Team acceptance affects not just the new employee's motivation, but the team's motivation as a whole. If your new candidate has any chance of negatively affecting team motivation, then they are not the right fit.

- **Have someone else interview the candidate**

In the same way that you share information with one person and not another, a candidate will do the same. The chemistry they have with you as the hiring manager may not be the same as with that of a second interviewer. You would be surprised what some candidates will share with someone else that could either make or break them. Think of it as getting a second opinion.

- **Trust your instincts**

Never try to make excuses for a candidate in order to make them fit the job requirements. Most if not all candidates are at their best when they attend an interview in terms of how they present themselves. Although instinct should not be your main deciding factor, it should definitely play a part in your decision making process. Your instincts about people are as important in your professional life as they are in your personal life.

- **Do not over sell the position to the candidate**

Remember that this is an interview. You want the candidate to sell themselves and their qualifications to you. Let them tell you why they think they are the best fit for the company and position, not the other way around. This is a very common mistake that could affect your decision and your ability to make the right choice. Give the candidate only the information they need to make an informed decision such as benefits, 401K, etc. There will be plenty of time to sell the company after the candidate is hired.

Once you make a decision to hire the candidate, you want to make sure that their first day goes as smoothly as possible. Several things need to be accomplished to make this happen.

The new employee will be excited about their first day and will share their experience with others. You want what they share to be positive because you will eventually have to fill future job openings. Start by making sure you have everything ready for the employee when they come in. Complete the pre-start checklist below to ensure that you are not forgetting anything.

PRE-START CHECKLIST

ITEM	PRE-START CHECKLIST	YES	NO
1.	Offer letter signed and returned to HR.	☐	☐
2.	Office space available.	☐	☐
3.	If not, office space arrangements made.	☐	☐
4.	Computer/laptop with all necessary access requested.	☐	☐
5.	Employee's email is set up.	☐	☐
6.	Phone and phone number assignment requested.	☐	☐
7.	Building access key requested (if necessary).	☐	☐
8.	Ordered necessary supplies - pads, pens, stapler, calculator, tape, hole punch, etc.	☐	☐
9.	Employee is enrolled in the next new hire orientation session.	☐	☐
10.	Called employee to confirm start date and time.	☐	☐

5 THINGS TO AVOID ON THE EMPLOYEE'S FIRST DAY:

1. Do not send someone to meet the employee in the lobby on your behalf unless there are extenuating circumstances that prevent you from doing so.
2. Do not neglect to introduce the new employee to the team. This helps the employee acclimate faster and allows them to feel more comfortable asking for help.
3. If the new hire orientation does not fall on their start date, do not neglect to give them or arrange for a building tour.
4. Do not neglect to provide the employee with office space and supplies on their first day.
5. Do not ask the employee to call Technical Support and check on the status of their new computer/laptop/phone if delayed.

These mistakes could demotivate your employees very early in the game and prevent them from reaching productivity quickly. You want to avoid these issues at all costs.

2.0 ORIENTATION

In geometry, orientation is the placement of an object in a rotational coordinate system with respect to a reference position. Think about that for a moment. Think about some of the projects you have had to work on, in your professional or personal life. How important was it for you to have a point of reference? A point of reference guides your project and ensures that you do not go astray. If you, as a manager, do not provide the new employee with a point of reference, they have nothing to go on. A new employee may have experience in the industry, but they do not have the information they need to fit in to the company culture and in turn the departmental culture.

Giving an employee a point of reference lets you harness their desire to learn and perform at their full potential. During the first few days with the company, enroll them in the next available orientation session. If your company does not have an official orientation process, like many smaller businesses, it is still imperative to orient the new employee. Use your office or a conference room to deliver information to the new employee. Work with HR or another company representative to provide your new employee with basic information about the company, including:

- Company history
- Benefits and HR policy information
- Basic product or service offering information
- Basic system overview if the company uses one system/database to store information

Do not deny your employee the opportunity to learn. Managers often hire reactively such that once that employee accepts an offer, they are immediately put to work with absolutely no formal orientation or training.

In running an orientation program myself, I learned that new hires greatly valued the information they received during orientation. When employees don't get the opportunity to attend orientation they feel deprived of important information about their job. Remember that your employees' performance reflects on you. When training takes the back burner, your low-producing employees may end up teaching your new employee how it is done. The last thing you want is for a motivated new employee to be demotivated by a lack of appropriate training.

Once formed, bad habits are hard to break. Are you willing to take that chance? Are you prepared to deal with another low-producing employee? In order for your employee to feel welcome, stay motivated, and perform better than average, you need to ensure that they get the training they need. You did not have this employee working for you before now – what's a few more days? If you want your employee to reach seniority and not actively seek other employment while working for you, then you need to give them a reason to stay and a way that they can succeed with you!

ABOUT THE COMPANY

Think about the information you received the last time you started a new job. Now think about how it affected your attitude toward your job responsibilities and the company as a whole. You had either a positive experience or a negative one.

In the orientation session, the candidate should receive basic information about the company. When, where, and by whom was the company founded? What market is serviced? How many locations and employees are there? Has the company been nominated for or received any awards? Who are the members of the executive team?

It is important to spend time talking about the company because this is a good time to sell the new employee on their employer. You do not want them to change their mind about taking the position or accept another position while working for you.

WHAT ARE MY BENEFITS?

In most companies, new employees receive the necessary benefit forms early in the hiring process. Orientation is a great time to provide detailed information on the benefits offered and for the new employee to pose any questions they have to HR personnel.

HR POLICIES

Encourage employees to take as much advantage of the HR session as possible. This is when employees get information on what is acceptable and what is not, including information on the consequences of unacceptable behavior. Issues such as dress code, sexual harassment, whistle blowing, and confidentiality are key policies that any new employee needs to understand. The employee should leave orientation with a thorough appreciation of what the company expects from them and what they should expect from the company.

Having the employee spend some time with an HR representative does not mean you are off the hook. Your department or team has policies that need to be discussed. Once the company polices are out of the way, you as the manager need to talk with the employee about your particular departments' policies:

- **Attendance:** What are the employee's hours? Discuss consequences of tardiness if any.
- **Breaks:** How many breaks per day, and how long should each break last?
- **Time off:** How should time off be requested, and what type of advance notice is required?
- **Probation:** How long is the probationary period, and how is the employee reviewed during and after this period? Most probationary periods are 60–90 days from the date of hire.
- **Metrics:** This is a topic that is often forgotten. Discuss with the employee how they will be measured, not only during probation but going forward. How are they rated on performance on a daily, weekly, or monthly basis? Is their performance tied to a bonus? It's important to discuss with the employee the actions required to attain the top performance metrics. Ensure that you provide the metrics to them in writing so that they can reference them often. Let them know that they will be reviewed on those metrics once their training is complete.
- **Annual reviews:** Discuss how their performance affects their annual reviews and raises if applicable.

WHAT PRODUCTS/SERVICES DOES THE COMPANY PROVIDE?

Sales personnel are not the only ones who require product or service information. If customer satisfaction is one of the important key performance indicators for the company, then product and/or service knowledge should be as well. All employees should get this information, in varying detail, based on their position and how often they need to reference this information on a daily basis.

> ***A person can only perform as well as the knowledge they have.***

Here's why - a person can only perform as well as the knowledge they have. Knowledge about the products or services provides the new employee an opportunity to perform at their best.

For example, if you hire operations personnel whose job is to place orders with vendors yet fail to provide the employee information about the nature of the business, how productive do you really think they will be?

If an employee thinks that a specific piece of information would help them do their job better, they are more likely to perform under par as long as they are lacking that information. Educate your employees on the nature of the business. A high-level overview is all it takes.

WHAT SYSTEMS ARE USED TO STORE CUSTOMER INFORMATION?

Most companies have a number of systems or databases used by different teams within the company. More often than not, one specific customer relationship management system is used by the majority (if not all) of the company. This is the system that needs to be reviewed with new hires. You want to ensure that they can not only access this system but also navigate the system and the records contained therein. The goal of this session is to give the new employee a well-rounded background of the system to serve as a foundation for when they begin their in-depth, job-specific training.

3.0
TRAINING AND DEVELOPMENT

After the new employee has some background information about the company and some high-level basics, it is important to educate them on how to perform their job successfully. Your goal is to groom that employee and give them all the information they need to reach their potential. If your employees succeed at their job, you succeed as well. If they successfully execute their tasks, you will meet your departmental goals and be successful!

Take some time to review your current on-boarding and on-the-job training process. How did you train your new hires in the past? What mistakes did you make? How can you improve? If your company documents exit interviews, review them for information that you can use to make your new employee's experiences better.

If your company allows it, look at exit interviews from employees in other departments you work with. The information you find will guide you towards keeping that new employee motivated and reduce churn by providing what others were lacking.

Some methods you could use to develop your employees include:

I. Shadowing

II. Formal Training

III. Workshops

IV. Book Clubs

I. SHADOWING

> ***Shadowing is not a bad thing; it's when you make it your only form of 'training' that it fails your new hire.***

Jessica had been working two full-time jobs, but the new position's salary replaced both. She left her day job but continued to work overnight for another week or so. After working all night, she was ready for the day and somewhat refreshed thanks to a much-needed caffeine boost. Her soda worked for the first hour or so, but as soon as she sat down for her shadowing session, it was downhill from there. Jessica tried to make sense of what was going on and stay awake, but there was no hope of gaining anything from a full day of shadowing. "Honestly, I had absolutely no idea what was going on," Jessica reported.

Joanne, the employee Jessica was shadowing, switched from one program to the next, picked up customer calls, complained to friends, responded to emails, and then went back to different programs. Jessica complained, "I couldn't take notes because nothing made sense, nor could I ask any questions because I didn't know where to begin." Joanne would occasionally say, "You should always do this," or "Never do that," and Jessica would write it down. Without the context and background knowledge of the process or the system, though, that information did her no good.

Ask yourself the following questions before you schedule a shadowing session:

1. How willing and able is the person being shadowed? Are they motivated and positive? Are they enthusiastic? Everyone has something to complain about, but a good employee will save it for later.
2. Does the person being shadowed have guidelines and a time frame for the session? Provide an outline of what you want them to focus on and assign specific tasks to meet your goal. For example, if you need the employee to cover order entry, assign them a new order to demonstrate in the session.
3. Does the new employee have any background knowledge to go on before the shadowing session? The employee being shadowed is more concerned about getting their work done, which means there will be more doing than explaining. It can be very overwhelming if the new employee has no idea why a task is being completed let alone how to complete it. They also cannot make sense of the order of events unless they have that foundational information.

Two full weeks after Jessica's start date, she finally received her first project, a task based on the information she had received during shadowing. Jessica had a million questions but no reference material except the notes she attempted to make during the shadowing sessions. To accomplish this task, Jessica felt like she wasted a lot of time seeking information that she would have received during a training session.

SUMMARY - 5 STEPS OF SHADOWING:

1. Ensure that the employee being shadowed is a top performer. The new employee should spend time with positive and productive people.
2. Select an employee with good interpersonal skills.
3. Schedule the shadowing session with a goal in mind. The session will be more beneficial if all parties involved have the same purpose.

4. Ensure that the employee has some background knowledge on the task they will be shadowing. This will enable them to grasp the finer details.

5. Don't forget about the employee. Come back and check on them often, especially if the session is more than an hour or two long. It is difficult to stay awake and focused if the session is too long and is not interactive.

> ***Shadowing should be incorporated into a formal training program to reinforce positive/ expected behavior.***

Any time you have to schedule a shadowing session, first cover the specific skill they will be shadowing. Then allow the employee to practice the skill in a test environment. Finally, have them watch the same skill performed in a live environment. Ask the employee being shadowed to focus on the specific skill for an hour or two and be sure to come back after that time frame to discuss with both employees what was learned.

Shadowing provides a way for your new employee to learn more and for your existing employee to cooperate and feel that they helped the new employee meet their learning goal.

II. FORMAL TRAINING

Develop a training program if you do not already have one. You do not have to be the one conducting the training; a good number of managers today are working managers, which means you may not have the time to train the new employee yourself. You must, however, be involved. Your involvement lets the new employee know that they are valuable to you and that you care about their success. You want your new employee to learn almost constantly for the first few months with the company.

To create a training program, you must have a current and accurate job description. You need to know the employee's daily tasks to ensure that they have all the information needed to get the job done. Review the job description and think sequentially. Break the knowledge up into logical pieces that will easily come together and make sense in the end. Your goal is to organize training topics in an orderly manner so that topic one, for example, is a prerequisite for topic two.

Call center scenario: developing a training program

Let's take the example of an employee who works in a call center. If the employee's job involves taking calls in order to respond to customer troubles, you need to ask yourself the following questions.

1. **What's the first thing to do when the call comes in?**

Information on etiquette, like any other information provided to the employees, should be documented. Scripts are the most common way to handle this situation. Keep in mind that the information you provide says a lot about the company, not just to the employee but also to those on the other end of the call. These scripts should contain statements that more or less describe company culture and the company's standing on customer satisfaction.

For example:

'Your call is very important to us.'

'I understand your frustration.'

'We strive to provide you with a state-of-the-art product/service.'

The employee needs training to know what questions to ask the customer, when they can place a customer on hold, how to stay calm, and so on. Never rule anything out as 'common sense.'

2. **What type of troubles do customers normally report?**

Ensure that the employee has both a list of commonly received troubles and a description of those troubles. If something does not work, what does that mean? How should it work? How can it be resolved? This is the time to essentially dig deeper into the product/service overview the employee received during orientation. Give them as much detail as necessary to ensure they are successful at their daily tasks.

Let's say that the company provides online bill pay and that the bill pay system includes a number of pop-up windows. A common problem may be a 'page not found' error message; the solution may be a triage of issues. For example, the first possible resolution would be to turn off the pop-up blocker. If that doesn't resolve the problem, the employee would be instructed to go to the second possible resolution.

3. **Which departments handle which specific issues?**

Expand the overview the new employee received during orientation. Focus on the departments that the employee will be working with and provide detail about what each one does in relation to the employee's job. Discuss the key players as well as the escalation procedures for each department. The employee needs to know about the intervals for specific tasks within each department and each level of escalation. Give your employee a copy of this information for reference.

4. **How quickly should the call be answered, and how long should an average call last?**

Call centers have statistics that affect customer satisfaction. Receivers are taught the importance of a low 'dropped call' percentage. Provide them with a chart of any such statistics. If the goal of a receiver is to handle the call as quickly as possible, then you as a manager should ensure that they have the appropriate knowledge to do so. You want them to answer those calls and quickly resolve the customer's problem using the knowledge provided to them in training.

Provide the employee with in-depth information about the systems and products/services provided, such as how they work and how they are fixed when broken. The more background information they have, the easier it is to diagnose problems.

5. **If the employee can resolve the trouble, what should they do?**

Discuss procedural items with the new employee. Many public companies must meet Sarbanes-Oxley compliance, commonly known as Sox or Sarbox, a federal law enacted in 2002 that requires publicly held companies and accounting firms to disclose financial information. It also requires documentation of all processes to ensure procedures are correctly followed and nothing slips through the cracks.

If a call comes in, is there a system for recording that information? If so, explain what it is and how to access it. What is the proper way to document the call? How do you resolve the customer's issue and document it? The employee can pull from the wealth of information they have already received about the products/services and how they work.

6. **If the employee cannot resolve the trouble, what should they do?**

Employees should do what they can based on the information they received about the products/services and how they work. Failing that, they refer the trouble to someone else to complete the resolution. If an issue is referred elsewhere for resolution, ensure the employee knows:

- The type of issue that should be referred to another individual or group.
- The individual or group that would receive each type of issue.
- The proper way to handle a call, such as:
    - » Transferring the call. Make sure they know to stay on the call with the customer during call transfer, and that they should and only hang up after the customer has been introduced to the person expected to resolve the issue.

» Opening a trouble report and keeping close contact with the customer regarding updates, even when none exist.

Training Agenda

The six steps above provided an example for thinking through creation of a training program for a call center employee. These steps, however, apply to any type of business group. In more general terms, your training agenda might resemble the following:

Item One. Overview of what's expected of the employee on a daily, weekly, monthly basis and how their performance affects the department and the company as a whole.

Item Two. In-depth product/service review as it relates to the employee's job. Keep this session job-specific. Employ both online learning modules if available as well as instructor-led sessions. Blended learning is very effective, as it covers a range of learning styles: visual, auditory, or both.

Item Three. Discuss how the job tasks relate to each other. Provide the employee with a step-by-step process and the sequence of these tasks, being sure to discuss each step/task in detail. Some tasks cannot be completed before others, so be sure to discuss this as well.

Item Four. Divulge system/database knowledge as it relates to the employee's job. Items Three and Four might need to be handled in parallel depending on the employee's tasks. For example, if the employee is a project coordinator, their first task might be to call the customer and introduce themselves. The second task may then be to document that call. In this instance, review what database should be used to document the activity as well as how the documentation should be completed.

Item Five. Discuss hypothetical or 'if/then' scenarios. If a customer changes their mind about a product or service, then what should the employee do? If the deadlines change, then how should they escalate or stall the process? If a customer has a problem with a product or service, then how would the employee report and/or track it? Provide as many scenarios as possible. This is a good time to incorporate a shadowing session so that your employees gain first-hand knowledge about the types of situations they will encounter on a daily basis. Let the employee spend time with one of the top performers in the group.

Item Six. Include hands-on exercises throughout the training, allowing the employee to perform some tasks by themselves whenever possible. Quiz them after the task in order to keep them engaged. Once they have the basic information, in as much detail as possible, allow them to work under supervision. Humans learn best by doing. At this stage, assign them some tasks and either supervise them closely or assign one of your senior team members to do so. The latter is probably the best option as it allows you some time to do your job and allows the employee to experience working with others on the team. Ensure that you are entrusting them to someone who does the job right, someone whose performance you are pleased with. Continue to assign supervised tasks until you observe their comfort level (and yours) at working alone.

SAMPLE 5-DAY TRAINING AGENDA		
Time	**Topic**	**Done**
Days One & Two		
9:00AM to 4:00PM	Orientation	☐
Day Three		
9:00AM to 10:00AM	Expectations	☐
10:00AM to 11:00AM	Web-Based Training (WBT) Product/Service Knowledge	☐
11:00AM to 12:00PM	Product/Service Knowledge (How to …)	☐
1:00PM to 2:00PM	Shadowing; Q&A	☐
2:00PM to 4:00PM	Product/Service Knowledge (How to …)	☐
Day Four		
9:00AM to 10:00AM	WBT Database Review	☐
10:00AM to 12:00PM	Database access, how it is used	☐
1:00PM to 4:00PM	Step-by-step processes e.g. Creating a customer account (Step 1, Step 2.) Troubleshooting (Step 1, Step 2.) Selling (Step 1, Step 2.)	☐
Day Five		
9:00AM to 11:00AM	Scenario-based review	☐
11:00AM to 12:00PM	Shadowing; Q&A	☐
1:00PM to 2:00PM	WBT-Basic Skills (e.g. communicating, listening)	☐
2:00PM to 4:00PM	Exam; Q&A	☐

III. WORKSHOPS

The workshop wasn't an entirely negative experience for Jessica like shadowing was. She talked about a workshop in which she learned a great deal: "Our team was divided up into groups of two. Each team was assigned a topic/system that we dealt with daily. We had to create a method of procedure for completing a certain task within two weeks. Each team had ten minutes to present their material at the workshop. The teams were judged on material, presentation style, time keeping, and overall effectiveness. The best performing team got a plaque."

Jessica's story illustrates that it is important to keep training sessions as interesting as possible. Many people have preconceived notions about training, so you need to get creative. Try structuring your training sessions like workshops. Workshops tend to be more interactive and allow participants to learn via real-life examples: situations that they themselves have or are currently experiencing. What's great about Jessica's workshop is that it fostered motivation through challenge, control and competition. It also provided documentation that could be used by other employees.

- **Challenge:** Jessica's workshop encouraged team members to work together towards a specific goal. The goal was clearly defined and had a specific date for completion.
- **Control:** The employees had control over how to organize their presentation and method of procedure. With 10 minutes to present, they had to decide whether to create one or two documents – the 10 minute presentation and/or a comprehensive method of procedure.
- **Competition:** The teams knew the judging criteria to win the plaque, so they focused on being successful.

Think about how you can use workshops to improve process documentation, team dynamics, and process knowledge across the organization.

IV. BOOK CLUBS

Yes, book clubs at work! Most managers today are working managers, leaving very little time for leadership and management activities or self-development. Starting a book club is an excellent way to encourage management teams to take on these extremely important tasks and to develop their skills as managers.

Managers might want to read books on leadership, performance, development, evaluations, and industry-related topics that keep them up-to-date with the competition. Don't be limited by the title of the club: articles and magazines are also useful. Different people have different reading preferences. Subscribe to management or industry magazines for your management team. Have your managers share articles from books or magazines and print articles for them to read each month for discussion during your management meetings. This will give your managers some time to develop themselves and learn from one another. Focus on constantly improving their leadership skills, as this will reflect in team performance. A good leader can bring out the best in their team members.

4.0
EVALUATION AND FOLLOW-UP

Training is not the same thing as learning. It is therefore important to ensure that your employees learn key information during training. Conducting an evaluation will give you information about the employee's preparedness and also reinforce the employee's knowledge. One way to review the employee's knowledge is to provide them with a quiz and/or project. If they fall short of the goal, reinforce the specific areas where weakness is observed and let them know that they have the opportunity to try again. Everyone deserves a second chance, and a lot of times it takes at least two tries to master a skill. Focus on conducting that evaluation on multiple levels: Reaction, Learning, Application, and Business Impact.

Everyone deserves a second chance, and a lot of times it takes at least two tries to master a skill.

REACTION:

Measuring participants' reaction to the training is probably the easiest type of evaluation and also the most commonly administered. Reaction is often evaluated after the completion of a program while all the information is still fresh in the participant's mind. It is important to get participant feedback on issues such as program duration, hands-on labs, content, handouts, and any other material used in the training.

Gauging an employee's reaction is important as it allows you to make any needed adjustments to the program. This type of assessment should be used for any training or informational sessions that last more than one hour. Shorter training sessions do not provide enough content for reactions to be valuable.

LEARNING:

The most common, informal way to measure learning is by providing simulations, assessments, exercises and/or role-playing. These activities can be undertaken immediately following a training session or anywhere from a few hours to a few days after the training session.

Keep in mind that this initial evaluation to measure learning does not tell you how well or whether the employee will apply the knowledge to their current job. It is therefore vital to take evaluation one step further, into application, to ensure that they retained the knowledge and that they understand how to apply that knowledge.

APPLICATION:

Measuring application is not an easy task, as it requires time and patience. Some of the ways to measure knowledge transfer include surveys, employee observation, assignments, and interviews. The key to getting the most accurate information is to provide the survey to or interview both the employee and someone who works closely with that employee. Once you have the results, whether favorable or unfavorable, focus on reinforcement.

As the employee's manager you have significant influence on the employee's behavior. You need to:

- Encourage them to use the skills they learned frequently.
- Help them identify problems in order to figure out if new skills are needed.
- Discuss alternatives to handling specific situations.
- Be a role model.
- Give positive rewards for proper use of skills.

Measuring Application Assessment

Use the following scale to indicate how well the new hire is applying the knowledge they learned.

1 = Not at all; 2 = Needs improvement; 3 = Satisfactory; 4 = Very good; 5 = Excellent

The goal is to identify what areas need improvement. Is it the actual skill, communication of the skill, or execution of the skill?

SAMPLE FOLLOW-UP QUESTIONNAIRE						
1.	Understands how to use the skill.	1	2	3	4	5
2.	Knows what reference material to refer to if needed.	1	2	3	4	5
3.	Confident about what is required.	1	2	3	4	5
4.	Produces great reports.	1	2	3	4	5
5.	Contributes at team meetings.	1	2	3	4	5
6.	Communicates well with (internal & external) customers.	1	2	3	4	5
7.	Works well independently.	1	2	3	4	5
8.	Uses problem solving skills where needed.	1	2	3	4	5
9.	Demonstrates analytical skills.	1	2	3	4	5
10.	Goes above and beyond what is required.	1	2	3	4	5

Interpreting the Results:

Actual skill – Add the score for questions 1-3.

Communication of the skill – Add the score for questions 4-7.

Execution of the skill - Add the score for questions 8-10.

- A score of 0-5 indicates that the employee does not have a clear understanding of what is required of them.
- A score of 5-10 indicates average performance; employee probably has an idea about what areas need improvement.
- A score of 10-20 indicates that the employee is comfortable with their job and can only get better.

In all cases, on-going performance feedback and coaching is necessary to help increase or maintain expected performance levels.

BUSINESS IMPACT:

It is important to measure business impact, which should be tied in to the individual and departmental goals that you previously discussed with your employee. You essentially want to measure how well they are meeting or exceeding those goals. Understanding the employees' job function and tailoring the training to that job function is therefore important. If you do not train on the right thing, you cannot expect the employee to have a positive effect on performance or productivity.

How well are they following procedure? Are they meeting their numbers? Are they working more independently now than they were 30 days prior?

When you measure business result, ensure that you provide yourself and the employee an ample timeframe before you measure business impact; for example, 30 to 60 days after the training.

Part Two:

WHAT'S IN IT FOR ME?

5.0 SELF-ACTUALIZATION

Jessica was working in retail before she made her career move. She loved her job in the jewelry store. She met a lot of different people, her colleagues and boss were easy-going, and the work environment was warm. There were a lot of good things about this company, a small, family-owned business with multiple locations. They had great recognition programs and yearly bonuses, but something was missing. There was no room for advancement. Jessica needed more. "I needed to know that there was an opportunity out there to aim for; that I was working towards something more; that I, as an individual, would be more accomplished in the next several months. I wanted more!" There are people in your organization just like Jessica who want more, and you need to identify who they are.

In the world of business today, there are two types of people. First are those who are satisfied in their positions and do not want to or need to advance, either because their personal lives do not allow for any schedule changes that may be caused by increased responsibility or because they are simply happy and do not want to leave their comfort zone. Then there are those who want to move as high up the ladder as their company will allow. Nurture them, provided their desire is not destructive to others. In most cases, these will be your most productive employees.

To unlock the potential of these high-achieving employees, you need to understand what they are looking for in terms of personal or professional development by discussing this during your one-on-one time with them. Find out where they want to be and discuss how they can get there. You want to avoid losing productive and loyal employees.

Abraham Maslow, founder of the discipline of humanistic psychology, suggested that everyone has a hierarchy of needs that must be met. These needs range from basic physiological needs to safety needs, social needs, esteem needs, and self-actualization. Once the lower-level basic needs are met, then a person will seek to meet his or her higher-level esteem and self-actualization needs.

Maslow described self-actualization as:

> "an episode or spurt in which the powers of the person come together in a particularly and intensely enjoyable way, and in which he is more integrated and less split, more open for experience, more idiosyncratic, more perfectly expressive or spontaneous, or fully functioning, more creative, more humorous, more ego-transcending, more independent of

his lower needs, etc. He becomes in these episodes more truly himself, more perfectly actualising his potentialities, closer to the core of his being, more fully human. Not only are these his happiest and most thrilling moments, but they are also moments of greatest maturity, individuation, fulfillment - in a word, his healthiest moments."

If for any reason an employee's lower needs are in jeopardy, they will be more concerned with trying to meet those needs before they concern themselves with higher-level needs. An employee who is sick or has lost a loved one, for example, will not be thinking about career advancement. This concern with low-level needs might manifest itself in decreased productivity, tardiness, or an increase in time off. You would be amazed how closely this hierarchy of needs applies to our day-to-day lives in the workplace.

MASLOW'S ORIGINAL HIERARCHY OF NEEDS

Self-Actualization	maturity, individuation, fulfillment
Esteem	achievement, confidence, mutual respect
Love/Belonging	family, friends, intimacy
Safety	security of property, family, employment
Physiological	food, water, sleep, sex

As human beings, we want personal development, not only at home but at work as well. Employees want challenges and opportunities for growth. They want to engage in activities that enhance or maintain their self-image. It is important to provide these in order to keep employees motivated. They need to know that they have the opportunity to self-actualize, to reach their potential, and that you can provide them with a challenging path to achieve it. In light of Maslow's definition of self-actualization, imagine how productive your employees would be if they were "...more open for experience, more idiosyncratic, more perfectly expressive or spontaneous, or fully functioning, more creative." Most employees respond to any opportunities for challenge, interesting work, and responsibility.

3 activities that enhance employees' self-image:

1. Development
2. Challenge
3. Empowerment

Development - Create opportunities for development by providing on-line learning opportunities such as self-paced on-line learning, live events and seminars, reading assignments, and projects that require research. You want the employee to be a continuous learning machine by stimulating their interest to learn more.

Challenge - Goals are important. Provide the employees with challenging but attainable goals to meet, and be sure to provide them with feedback on their performance. These goals should be meaningful and measurable. Creating difficult goals will only demotivate the employees. They will lose interest if they know that they cannot meet them.

Empowerment - Let the employees know that their work makes a difference and that the decisions they make affect not only them and their team, but the company as a whole.

PRACTICE 3: RECOGNITION

"No duty is more urgent than that of returning thanks."

-Unknown Author

Recognition is one of the most common ways to motivate employees, encourage them, and increase their interest in daily responsibilities. No one type of recognition will work in all situations. There are two forms: verbal and material recognition. Employees should be recognized for such things as:

1. Participating in educational experiences.
2. Individual progress toward goals.
3. Achievement of any established standards of excellence.
4. Results from healthy peer competition.

We often do not recognize the hard work that employees do on a daily basis. It is easier than you think to give verbal recognition. It does not take much to walk by their office or cubicle and say, "Hey, Kim, great work with that report today, it put everything in perspective and the turnaround was amazing." When giving verbal recognition, address the employee by name to personalize the conversation and take the time to tell that employee why you are recognizing their work. If you don't give a reason for the praise, it appears as though you don't mean it because you really don't know what they did. Make it your business to know what your employees are doing, especially when giving praise.

The same applies with material recognition, be it in the form of a bonus, plaque, theatre tickets, or dinner. Your employees need to know why they are being recognized. It tells them that you care, and it allows you to point out the good behavior that needs to be replicated.

Most important in giving praise is to do it as soon as you notice the action that deserves recognition, not a day or week or month later. Recognize the employee verbally immediately following the deserving action, then follow up with material rewards if you deem it necessary. Keep some free movie passes or company trinkets in your office or storage space to use as recognition rewards. Do not wait to give praise! It is a great feeling to have a boss who is so in touch with the employees' daily activities that they hardly miss what goes on.

You will not always be available to see employees' actions firsthand, but if you get wind of it be sure to recognize the employee as soon as you can.

PRACTICE 4: CAREER DEVELOPMENT

"The achievement of one goal should be the staring point of another."

-Alexander Graham Bell

Career development options provide more motivation than you might imagine. Employees want to know that there is opportunity for growth. They want to know that they will not be in the same position for the rest of their career. Some individuals don't want change, but the majority wants to grow in their positions.

As a manager, you should provide growth opportunities for your employees. Some of the opportunities may be in different teams or departments. Be sure to work with other managers to find out what's available in their departments and share what's available in yours.

STEPS TO CREATING A CAREER DEVELOPMENT PATH:

1. Create job descriptions for each position if you have not already done so. Job descriptions are important for hiring, training, and creating career paths, not to mention preventing lawsuits. Employees must have a clear understanding of their responsibilities.
2. Identify the different career development path options you would like to offer and outline their pay grades.
3. Set specific goals for each current position and outline any additional tasks that need to be completed in order to move to another position.
4. Outline what happens when they meet and/or exceed the requirements for each position.

JOB DESCRIPTION LAYOUT

Your position description statement should always indicate the opportunities that are available for that position, but you do not need to provide specific details on each of the positions. Keep an informational packet/handbook on the development opportunities handy. This packet should be available to your employees as a guide to success or a point of reference. In that packet, you should include:

1. The action that is required to move up or across to that position, including a timeline for goals or training.
2. The reason a development opportunity is either an upward move or a lateral move.
3. The salary increase, if applicable.
4. Whether or not a bonus accompanies the move.
5. The position description.
6. The application process or discussion required between manager and

employee before they undertake a specific opportunity.

Growth opportunities and job descriptions not only ensure that employees have a clear understanding of the goals they need to meet but also a clear understanding of the steps they need to take in order to attain the position they are seeking.

This knowledge of the 'light at the end of the tunnel' as well as the steps to get there keep employees motivated. Challenge your employees to reach or work towards reaching their potential.

Job Description

Position Objective:

The purpose of this position is to ensure both internal and external customer satisfaction by actively reaching out to customers. This position requires continuous tracking and measuring in order to ensure that customer satisfaction goals are being met.

Job Responsibilities:

- Conduct daily customer contacts and escalations
- Run weekly reports to track satisfaction; identify areas of improvement
- Document and communicate new processes to the rest of the team

60-Day Deliverables:

- Attend a 7-day training that includes New Hire Orientation
- Complete a Customer Satisfaction project within 2 weeks of hire
- Complete 10 online courses (Manager to provide list of courses required)
- Attain an 80% score in team metrics within 60 days of hire

Development Opportunities:

- Attend Customer Service seminar to improve skills
- Customer Service certification
- Team Lead certification

Opportunities for Growth:

- Team Lead
- Supervisor

Employee Signature: ______________________ Date: __________

Manager's Signature: ______________________ Date: __________

PRACTICE 5: COMMUNICATION

"In the old culture, managers got their power from secret knowledge: profit margins, market share, and all that... In the new culture, the role of the leader is to express a vision, get buy-in, and implement it. That calls for open, caring relations with every employee, and face-to-face communication."

- Jack Welch, in a letter to shareholders

6.0
TEAM MISSION

It is vital for employees to know that they are part of a winning team. The most effective way to do this is by communicating openly and often. You will find that most employees want to feel involved and informed; they want to belong to and develop relationships within the company.

The first thing you should communicate with your team is the company's mission and/or vision. You must then communicate the team's mission and how that ties in to the company's mission and/or vision. Many managers do not have a mission statement for their teams. Just as orientation as used in geometry relates to the placement of an object with respect to a fixed point or reference position, a mission statement creates a point of reference for your employees. This statement should be the team's reference point so that there is no question what is expected of them. Everyone is then on the same page at all times, following a mission statement as a guideline for processes, training, and development. Print it out, make a plaque of it, frame it if you dare, and put it in front of each of your employee's computer.

POINTS TO CONSIDER WHEN CREATING A MISSION STATEMENT

1. **What is a mission statement?**

A mission statement is like a brief statement of purpose. It is a myth that mission statements are only written by organizations. An individual or small group can use a mission statement to direct their personal and career paths as well.

2. **What should the mission statement include?**

What is your team's purpose? What do you desire to accomplish? What is the nature of your team's business? What are your team values and goals? If you can translate those four questions into a clear, concise statement that is free of jargon, you have a mission statement. Answering those questions will let others know what your team is about and how you do business.

Take a look at these sample mission statements:

Call Center

To respond to customer calls within five minutes and aim to resolve their issue on the first call as quickly as possible while providing a memorable experience.

- **Purpose:** to respond to customer calls within five minutes.
- **Business:** to resolve their issue on the first call.
- **Values/goals:** to provide a memorable experience.

Food Court

To provide the most satisfying meal to our customers by creating a meal filled with exciting flavors, full-bodied aromas, and delightful creations. We aim to provide a great atmosphere for external and internal customers alike.

- **Purpose:** to provide the most satisfying meal.
- **Business:** to create a meal filled with exciting flavors, full-bodied aromas, and delightful creations.
- **Values/goals:** provide a great atmosphere for external and internal customers alike.

Cleaning Service

Can you say, "No more dust under the rug?" You sure can with our cleaning service. No stone is left unturned. Our mission is to leave everything spotless and exactly where we found it. We also believe in order and can help you de-clutter.

- **Purpose:** to leave everything spotless and exactly where we found it.
- **Business:** to clean, leaving no stone unturned.
- **Values/goals:** to help restore order.

7.0
PART OF THE TEAM

The next thing you should communicate is information about the employee's individual performance.

Jessica was off to a shaky start but was hanging in there. She took it upon herself to learn the industry. Jessica spent time with her very knowledgeable supervisor and completed many of the self-paced on-line courses available. Each week, Jessica's supervisor met with her one-on-one about her projects, performance, and expectations. Had he not done this, Jessica probably would have lost both her motivation for self improvement and her desire to reach her potential and perform at her best.

Employees like to be informed about their performance. They want to know how they rank against the goals set for them as well as against their colleagues. They also want to know how their work affects the company as a whole.

Employees can feel lost due to lack of communication, direction, or support. Have you ever felt like no one really cared about what your responsibilities were or how you accomplished them? Working managers today have more non-managerial responsibilities and goals to meet than ever and are left with very little time to actually manage their employees or even to meet with them face-to-face individually or as a team. Lack of direction hinders performance and demotivates employees. It is impossible for an employee to reach their potential if there is no drive to do so.

One-on-one meetings are very effective. This is a time when you can discuss the employee's concerns, performance, and expectations. It is a time for open discussion, a time to provide the employee some guidelines and goals to meet within a given month or quarter. The frequency with which you meet with your team members depends on their responsibilities. A customer service manager may need to meet with their team more often than a field services manager.

In thinking about employee performance, keep in mind that you should:

- Conduct team meetings to encourage open communication.
- Meet with your direct reports one-on-one and determine whether, as part of their goals, they should meet with their direct reports.

- Ensure that the same message is communicated from top to bottom.
- Make random appearances at a couple one-on-ones conducted by each of your direct reports.
- Ensure that all one-on-one meetings are documented.

ONE-ON-ONE DOCUMENTATION TEMPLATE

(Some HR departments have templates that you can use)

Employee: ______________________________ Date: ____________

Metrics:

GOAL	% OF GOAL MET

Development Opportunities:

GOAL	DATE COMPLETED

Employee's Concerns:

1. ____
2. ____
3. ____
4. ____
5. ____
6. ____

Employee Signature: ______________________________ Date: ____________

Manager's Signature: ______________________________ Date: ____________

8.0
EMPLOYEE PARTICIPATION

Employee participation is extremely important in the workplace. There are various ways to encourage participation that will result in an increased sense of belonging as well as an increase in employees' self-esteem. Four ways that you can foster participation are outlined below.

I. SUGGESTIONS

Many companies have some type of suggestion process where they encourage employees to submit their thoughts about the company or about existing processes and products. Some companies will reward employees for making winning suggestions, such as those that lead to more streamlined processes, increased revenue, increased productivity, and higher customer satisfaction.

> ***Your employees should feel that they are part of the process and that they have an impact within the company.***

Pilot or focus groups can also be used to test new systems or products as they relate to the employee's job. For example, software engineers or developers can employ a pilot group as a great way to receive user interface feedback before launching a new application. Focus groups provide a marketing team with feedback about a product before its launch to a new market.

Your employees should feel that they are part of the process and that they have an impact within the company. In some situations, it may be necessary to outsource this kind of feedback. Any situation in which employees can assist such groups within the company, however, allows you to:

1. Cut the costs of outsourced focus groups.
2. Motivate and increase employee self-esteem.

II. ORGANIZED GROUPS

Organized groups can be sponsored by the employer but should be created and run by employees. Some organized groups of employees include book clubs, diversity groups, and sports groups such as bowling or softball leagues. Human Resources should define all rules relating to how these groups represent the company. Outside of that, though, employees should be allowed to set the group membership rules (non-discriminatory), the benefits of being in the group, and the meeting or practice sessions (outside of business hours). There are several companies that have these types of groups. Take Jessica for example. When she learnt about a softball league at her company, she joined the team as she enjoyed extracurricular activities. There she had a chance to meet employees from different teams and make valuable connections during practice and team events. These connections improved interaction among the team members during business hours. As a result, the employees on the softball team were better able to contribute to each other's job tasks and support each other as they had learnt to do out in the field.

III. COMMUNITY SERVICE

Involvement in community service gives your employees a change of environment while representing your team or company in the community. Not all employees will participate in community service projects, so you should never make it mandatory. Those that are interested in community service will jump at the opportunity. Most businesses today, whether small or large, are involved with senior centers, local charities that host walking, running or golfing events, Red Cross blood drives, and mentor programs. There are a lot of options, but a little research is all it takes to find the perfect community service project for your organization. Getting involved in community service builds not only your employees' character but the company's as well. It is also a great opportunity to advertise your business.

IV. COMPANY EVENTS

A change in the working environment can be as good as a rest for your employees. Company events are a great way to encourage networking and communication across the company. You can also use this opportunity to involve employees' families in their work life. Much of your employees' time is spent at work, and many have very little free time to spend with their families.

Some companies tend to shy away from these events because they are afraid of losing valuable employee time or because of the expense associated with hosting an event. However, you can organize simple events and schedule them in such a way that your employees remain available by email or voicemail.

A few hours could keep you from losing valuable employees and could motivate them; motivated employees produce more than unmotivated ones. You can let your employees know that you care not only about them but also about their family by setting up events like:

1. **Bring-your-child-to-work Day.** This event allows children to be exposed to the work environment and their parent's day. Parents will enjoy the few hours they get to spend in the office with their children, and the children will enjoy seeing this place that their parents go to

every day. The best time to do this is usually when focus, production, and business in general are slower; Friday afternoons, for example.

2. **Holiday Events.** Some companies have a themed party or lunch for Halloween. Others encourage their employees to have a costume competition judged based on photos posted on the company's intranet. Other companies allow parents to bring their children to work in their Halloween costumes for a trick or treat event. For other events, companies might provide green cookies or shakes for St. Patrick's Day or red for Valentine's Day.
3. **Sporting Events.** Employees can wear their favorite player's jersey on opening day, for example. If cost is not too much of a concern, a tailgate lunch can be served.
4. **Christmas Parties.** This could be an in-company lunch or a dinner party that includes spouses and significant others. Similar to the Halloween event, employees could be encouraged to decorate their space, and winners would be selected based on specific judging criteria.

CONCLUSION

How do you unlock an employee's hidden potential? Watch, listen, and learn. Understand what employees are looking for when they come in the door. To successfully meet your business needs, you need to focus on the needs of your employees as well. Strive to answer their biggest question, 'What's in it for me?' Then go one step further to ensure that the performance of your employees supports the performance of your business objectives.

It is very important for managers to realize that their success is not a one-way street. You are the boss and employees should take direction from you, but you must prioritize understanding your employees in order to provide an environment that fosters motivation, productivity, and creativity. How you treat your employees has an effect on how they respond to your direction. Neglecting the needs of your employees is detrimental to your organization's success. Employees whose needs are not met can cause rebellion, which may be either subtle or overt. Subtle rebellion includes, but is not limited to:

Watch, listen, and learn from your employees, industry experts, and competitors. You can't know it all.

- Lack of participation;
- Mediocre performance;
- Poor attendance;
- Poor quality of work;
- Decreased respect for you, co-workers, and company.

Show your employees the same respect you would like them to show you. Take the time to bring out the good, the smart, and the creative in them so they can work at their full potential.

1. Think about what you want to accomplish and create a plan to get there.
2. Make it your goal to hire motivated employees that fit the job description and culture as closely as possible.
3. Find out what motivates your existing employees.
4. Focus on providing an environment that fosters motivation and instills the kind of confidence that encourages performance improvement.
5. Provide in-depth training for new hires. Create a learning environment that encourages your employees to seek knowledge beyond what is required of them. This will give them the opportunity to develop themselves, build confidence, and increase their self-esteem.
6. Allow room for advancement by creating opportunities or internal certifications for them. Let them feel that there is more to their job than just the daily routine.
7. Encourage networking and frequent communication through team meetings, learning events, and team-building exercises.
8. Take the time to earnestly recognize and reward good behavior.
9. Provide performance improvement plans where necessary.
10. Be patient and don't lose heart. It will take time to change your work environment, but it is possible.

The five best practices are: Motivation, On-boarding, Recognition, Career Development, and Communication. The methods and implementation of these practices may be different for each organization. Understanding your business objectives, your employees, and these practices will allow you to retain your most talented and productive employees. By focusing on addressing the five best practices outlined in this book, you will be able to give a thorough answer when your employees ask, "What's in it for me?"

BIOGRAPHY

Njanja Mathu-Gakuru is a Learning and Development professional with extensive experience in management and corporate training. She creates and facilitates New Hire Orientation and job enhancement training programs. She also designs course content for E-Learning and Instructor-Led Training programs. Njanja coordinates leadership development, career development and workforce collaboration efforts. She has a Bachelor of Arts degree in Psychology with a minor in Management and has published several articles on employee performance, engagement and productivity. Her education, work with all levels of employees, management experience and insight into what matters to both employees and management provided the basis for this book.

INDEX

APPENDIX

SAMPLE TRAINING AGENDA

SAMPLE 5-DAY TRAINING AGENDA		
TIME	**TOPIC**	**DONE**
DAYS ONE & TWO		
9:00AM to 4:00PM	Orientation	☐
DAY THREE		
9:00AM to 10:00AM	Expectations	☐
10:00AM to 11:00AM	Web-Based Training (WBT) Product/Service Knowledge	☐
11:00AM to 12:00PM	Product/Service Knowledge (How to …)	☐
1:00PM to 2:00PM	Shadowing; Q&A	☐
2:00PM to 4:00PM	Product/Service Knowledge (How to …)	☐
DAY FOUR		
9:00AM to 10:00AM	WBT Database Review	☐
10:00AM to 12:00PM	Database access, how it is used	☐
1:00PM to 4:00PM	Step-by-step processes e.g. Creating a customer account (Step 1, Step 2.) Troubleshooting (Step 1, Step 2.) Selling (Step 1, Step 2.)	☐
DAY FIVE		
9:00AM to 11:00AM	Scenario-based review	☐
11:00AM to 12:00PM	Shadowing; Q&A	☐
1:00PM to 2:00PM	WBT-Basic Skills (e.g. communicating, listening)	☐
2:00PM to 4:00PM	Exam; Q&A	☐

MEASURING APPLICATION ASSESSMENT

Use the following scale to indicate how well the new hire is applying the knowledge they learned. The goal is to identify what areas need improvement. Is it the actual skill, communication of the skill, or execution of the skill?

1 = Not at all; 2 = Needs improvement; 3 = Satisfactory; 4 = Very good; 5 = Excellent

Sample Follow-up Questionnaire						
1.	Understands how to use the skill.	1	2	3	4	5
2.	Knows what reference material to refer to if needed.	1	2	3	4	5
3.	Confident about what is required.	1	2	3	4	5
4.	Produces great reports.	1	2	3	4	5
5.	Contributes at team meetings.	1	2	3	4	5
6.	Communicates well with (internal & external) customers.	1	2	3	4	5
7.	Works well independently.	1	2	3	4	5
8.	Uses problem solving skills where needed.	1	2	3	4	5
9.	Demonstrates analytical skills.	1	2	3	4	5
10.	Goes above and beyond what is required.	1	2	3	4	5

INTERPRETING THE RESULTS:

- Actual skill – Add the score for questions 1-3.
- Communication of the skill – Add the score for questions 4-7.
- Execution of the skill - Add the score for questions 8-10.

A score of 0-5 indicates that the employee does not have a clear understanding of what is required of them.

A score of 5-10 indicates average performance; employee probably has an idea about what areas need improvement.

A score of 10-20 indicates that the employee is comfortable with their job and can only get better.

SAMPLE JOB DESCRIPTION

JOB DESCRIPTION	
Position Objective:	
Job Responsibilities: • • • **60-Day Deliverables:** • • • **Development Opportunities:** • • • **Opportunities for Growth:** • •	
Employee Signature: ______________________	Date: __________
Manager's Signature: ______________________	Date: __________

ONE-ON-ONE DOCUMENTATION

ONE-ON-ONE DOCUMENTATION TEMPLATE

(Some HR departments have templates that you can use)

Employee: ______________________________ Date: ____________

Metrics:

GOAL	% OF GOAL MET

Development Opportunities:

GOAL	DATE COMPLETED

Employee's Concerns:

1. ____
2. ____
3. ____
4. ____
5. ____
6. ____

Employee Signature: ______________________________ Date: ____________

Manager's Signature: ______________________________ Date: ____________

SUMMARY

Did you ever wonder what you could do to improve your employees' success within your team or company? In this easy-read book, you will gain insight into the five basic practices that matter to your employees and how implementing these can not only improve employee performance and retention but also impact your bottom line. These strategies are easy to implement and can be done right away with no associated costs. All it takes is sensitivity to the needs of your employees and a desire to effect change. Templates are provided as signposts along the way to help you start implementing these strategies.

PRAISE FOR WHAT'S IN IT FOR ME?

"The book is very good, it is a very easy read, is current and practical to any manager of a team. The templates make for immediate application. The book contains a good summary on what a manager should remember to do when orienting a new member. Mainly because one can be so busy and ignore those critical early steps that help place a new employee in new footing."

- Rhoda Gathoga, Research Director, Global Scripture Impact.

"In this book, Njanja has clearly articulated in very comprehensive terms, what every small and large business should know and do regarding human resource practices. From hiring to induction, training to team building, conflict resolution to succession planning, this book will teach you all those things you thought you knew and set your company up for success.

If you are looking to realign your company's human resource practices and beyond, to invest in your workforce, to improve retention and ultimately your success as an organization, I highly recommend this book. This is a great read for every employer - an absolute must."

-Joe Njoroge, B.A, M.S. Chief Operating Officer.

www.ingramcontent.com/pod-product-compliance
Lightning Source LLC
LaVergne TN
LVHW050940080826
845145LV00004B/1349

* 9 7 8 0 6 1 5 5 1 0 0 6 4 *